W9-AUS-075

Los Angeles

by Joyce Markovics

Consultant: Karla Ruiz, MA
Teachers College, Columbia University
New York, New York

BEARPORT
PUBLISHING

New York, New York

Credits

Cover, © Andrew Zarivny/Shutterstock; TOC Left, © Michael Urmann/Shutterstock; TOC Right, © Iryna Rasko/Shutterstock; 4–5, © Ron_Thomas/iStock; 7, © Sean Pavone/Shutterstock; 8, © hammett79/Shutterstock; 9, © Nserrano/CC BY-SA 3.0; 10L, © Aurora Photos/Alamy Stock Photo; 10–11, © oneinchpunch/iStock; 12T, © Alex Staroseltsev/Shutterstock; 12B, © City of Angels/Shutterstock; 13, © Sean Pavone/Shutterstock; 14–15, © bannosuke/Shutterstock; 16, © breazey/iStock; 17, © gregobagel/iStock; 18L, © oneinchpunch/Shutterstock; 18–19, © JonathanNicholls/iStock; 19R, © Philip Pilosian/Shutterstock; 20–21, © Martin Shields/Alamy Stock Photo; 21BL, © Alex Millauer/Shutterstock; 22 (Clockwise from Top Right), © trekandshoot/Shutterstock, © littleny/Shutterstock, © Zack Frank/Shutterstock, © Lynne Albright/Shutterstock, and © dszc/iStock; 23 (T to B), © Ken Wolter/Shutterstock, © LuFeeTheBear/Shutterstock, © Wolterk/iStock, © AlinaMD/Shutterstock, and © stigmatize/Shutterstock; 24, © Andrew Zarivny/Shutterstock.

Publisher: Kenn Goin
Senior Editor: Joyce Tavolacci
Creative Director: Spencer Brinker
Photo Researcher: Thomas Persano

Library of Congress Cataloging-in-Publication Data

Names: Markovics, Joyce L., author.
Title: Los Angeles / by Joyce Markovics.
Description: New York, New York : Bearport Publishing, 2018. | Series: Citified! | Audience: Ages 5 to 8. | Includes bibliographical references and index.
Identifiers: LCCN 2017005119 (print) | LCCN 2017007383 (ebook) | ISBN 9781684022311 (library bound) | ISBN 9781684022854 (Ebook)
Classification: LCC F869.L84 M35 2018 (print) | LCC F869.L84 (ebook) | DDC 979.4/94—dc23
LC record available at https://lccn.loc.gov/2017005119

For more information, write to Bearport Publishing Company, Inc., 45 West 21st Street, Suite 3B, New York, New York 10010. Printed in the United States of America.

10 9 8 7 6 5 4 3 2 1

Contents

Welcome to

Los Angeles

The City of Angels!

Los Angeles is Spanish for "The Angels."

5

Los Angeles is a big city in Southern California.

It covers 503 square miles (1,303 sq km).

Nearly 4 million people live there!

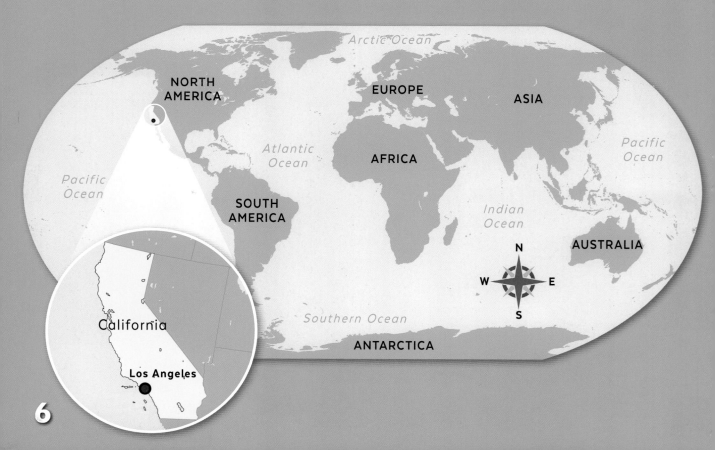

Los Angeles is called "LA" for short.

LA sits along the coast of the Pacific Ocean.

The city is surrounded on three sides by mountains.

Pacific Ocean

San Gabriel Mountains

Parts of the city are hilly, while other parts are flat.

People love LA's weather.

Almost every day is sunny and warm.

The average temperature is 64°F (18°C).

Only about 15 inches (38 cm) of rain falls in LA each year. That's half the national average.

Lights. Camera. Action!

Los Angeles is famous for its **film industry**.

Each year, hundreds of movies are made there.

On a hill above LA is the famous Hollywood sign.

It's 350 feet (107 m) long.

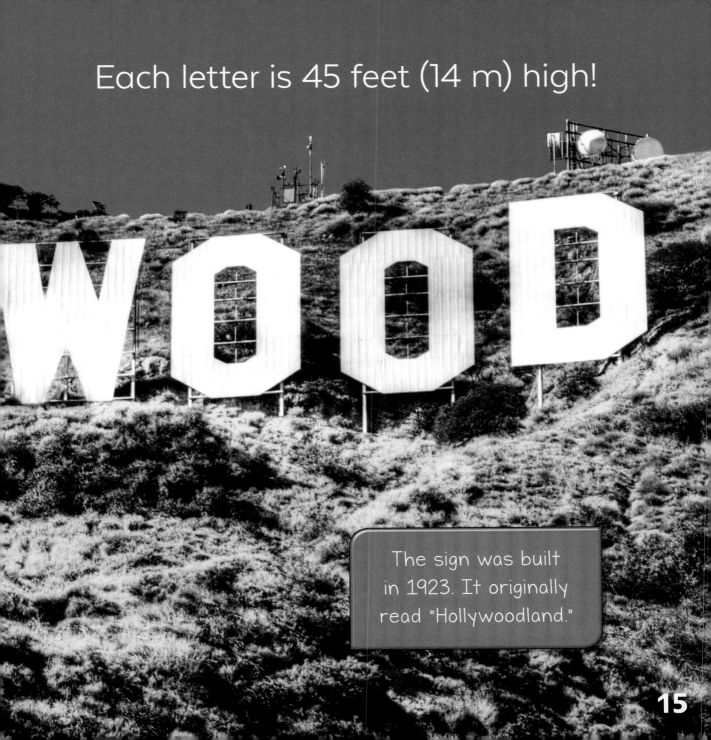

Each letter is 45 feet (14 m) high!

The sign was built in 1923. It originally read "Hollywoodland."

Los Angeles is home to **sprawling** Griffith Park.

People hike the park's many trails.

Griffith Park covers 4,310 acres (1,744 ha).

Some of the trails lead to an **observatory**.

At night, visitors can gaze at the stars!

Griffith Observatory

LA's Venice Beach draws lots of visitors.

Surfers come to ride the waves.

Skateboarders soar through the air.

Near Venice Beach is a **solar**-powered Ferris wheel!

What else is great about LA?

mammoth skeleton

The city has close to 100 museums.

Visit the La Brea Tar Pits museum.

It holds the **fossils** of millions of animals.

Come see why so many people love Los Angeles!

Thousands of years ago, giant mammoths roamed LA. Many died when they got stuck in pits filled with sticky tar.

MAP IT!
Los Angeles

CALIFORNIA

San Gabriel Mountains

Griffith Park

La Brea Tar Pits and Museum

MARILYN MONROE

Hollywood

Pacific Ocean

Cool Fact:
The Hollywood Walk of Fame is a long sidewalk covered with more than 2,500 stars. Each star has the name of a famous person on it.

Venice Beach

film industry (FILM IN-duh-*stree*) all of the businesses and companies that make movies

fossils (FOSS-uhlz) the remains or traces of plants and animals that lived a long time ago

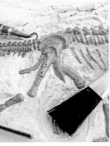

observatory (uhb-ZUR-vuh-*tor*-ee) a place for viewing stars and planets

solar (SOH-lur) having to do with the sun

sprawling (SPRAWL-ing) spreading out

Index

Read More

Duffield, Katy S.
*California History for
Kids.* Chicago: Chicago
Review Press (2012).

Yasuda, Anita. *What's Great
About California? (Our Great
States).* Minneapolis, MN:
Lerner (2014).

Learn More Online

To learn more about Los Angeles, visit
www.bearportpublishing.com/Citified

About the Author

Joyce Markovics lives along the Hudson
River in a very old house. She loves escaping
to Los Angeles to visit her little pal Luca.